HARD TIMES

Charles Dickens

EDITORIAL DIRECTOR Laurie Barnett
DIRECTOR OF TECHNOLOGY Tammy Hepps

SERIES EDITOR John Crowther
MANAGING EDITOR Vincent Janoski

WRITERS Brian Phillips, Juliet Shields
EDITORS Dennis Quinio, John Crowther

SPARKNOTES is a registered trademark of SparkNotes LLC

This edition published by Spark Publishing

Spark Publishing
A Division of SparkNotes LLC
120 Fifth Avenue, 8th Floor
New York, NY 10011

Please send all comments and questions or report errors to www.sparknotes.com/errors

Printed and bound in the United States

ISBN 1-58663-446-1

INTRODUCTION: STOPPING TO BUY SPARKNOTES ON A SNOWY EVENING

Whose words these are you *think* you know.
Your paper's due tomorrow, though;
We're glad to see you stopping here
To get some help before you go.

Lost your course? You'll find it here.
Face tests and essays without fear.
Between the words, good grades at stake:
Get great results throughout the year.

Once school bells caused your heart to quake
As teachers circled each mistake.
Use SparkNotes and no longer weep,
Ace every single test you take.

Yes, books are lovely, dark, and deep,
But only what you grasp you keep,
With hours to go before you sleep,
With hours to go before you sleep.

CONTENTS

CONTEXT

CHARLES DICKENS WAS BORN on February 7, 1812, and spent the first nine years of his life in Kent, a marshy region by the sea in the west of England. Dickens's father, John, was a kind and likable man, but he was incompetent with money and piled up tremendous debts throughout his life. When Dickens was nine, his family moved to London, and later, when he was twelve, his father was arrested and taken to debtors' prison. Dickens's mother moved his seven brothers and sisters into prison with their father but arranged for Charles to live alone outside the prison, working with other children at a nightmarish job in a blacking warehouse, pasting labels on bottles. The three months he spent apart from his family were highly traumatic for Dickens, and his job was miserable—he considered himself too good for it, earning the contempt of the other children.

After his father was released from prison, Dickens returned to school. He tried his hand professionally as a law clerk and then a court reporter before becoming a novelist. His first novel, *The Pickwick Papers,* became a huge popular success when Dickens was only twenty-five; he was a literary celebrity throughout England for the remainder of his life. At about this time, he fell in love with Mary Beadnell, the daughter of a banker. In spite of his ambition and literary success, Dickens was considered her social inferior in terms of wealth and family background, and Mary's father prohibited the marriage. Several years later, Dickens married Catherine Hogarth. Although they had ten children, Dickens was never completely happy in this marriage, and he and Catherine eventually separated.

Though the young blacking factory employee had considered himself too good for his job, the older novelist retained a deep interest in and concern for the plight of the poor, particularly poor children. The Victorian England in which Dickens lived was fraught with massive economic turmoil, as the Industrial Revolution sent shockwaves through the established order. The disparity between the rich and poor, or the middle and working classes, grew even greater as factory owners exploited their employees in order to increase their own profits. Workers, referred to as "the Hands" in *Hard Times,* were forced to work long hours for low pay in cramped, sooty, loud, and dangerous factories. Because they lacked education and job skills, these workers had few options for improving their terrible living and working conditions. With the empathy he gained through his own experience of poverty, Dickens became involved with a number of organizations that worked to alleviate the horrible living conditions of the London poor. For instance, he was a speaker for the Metropolitan Sanitary Organization, and, with his wealthy friend Angela Burdett-Coutts, he organized projects to clear up the slums and build clean, safe, cheap housing for the poor.

Though he was far too great a novelist to become a propagandist, Dickens several times used his art as a lens to focus attention on the plight of the poor and to attempt to awaken the conscience of the reader. *Hard Times* is just such a novel: set amid the industrial smokestacks and factories of Coketown, England, the novel uses its characters and stories to expose the massive gulf between the nation's rich and poor and to criticize what Dickens perceived as the unfeeling self-interest of the middle and upper classes. Indeed, *Hard Times* suggests that nineteenth-century England itself is turning into a factory machine: the middle class is concerned only with making a profit in the most efficient and practical way possible. *Hard Times* is not a delicate book: Dickens hammers home his point with vicious, often hilarious satire and sentimental melodrama. It is also not a difficult book: Dickens wanted all his readers to catch his point exactly, and the moral theme of the novel is very explicitly articulated time and again. There are no hidden meanings in *Hard Times,* and the book is an interesting case of a great writer subordinating his art to a moral and social purpose. Even if it is not Dickens's most popular novel, it is still an important expression of the values he thought were fundamental to human existence.

Plot Overview

THOMAS GRADGRIND, A WEALTHY, RETIRED MERCHANT in the industrial city of Coketown, England, devotes his life to a philosophy of rationalism, self-interest, and fact. He raises his oldest children, Louisa and Tom, according to this philosophy and never allows them to engage in fanciful or imaginative pursuits. He founds a school and charitably takes in one of the students, the kindly and imaginative Sissy Jupe, after the disappearance of her father, a circus entertainer.

As the Gradgrind children grow older, Tom becomes a dissipated, self-interested hedonist, and Louisa struggles with deep inner confusion, feeling as though she is missing something important in her life. Eventually Louisa marries Gradgrind's friend Josiah Bounderby, a wealthy factory owner and banker more than twice her age. Bounderby continually trumpets his role as a self-made man who was abandoned in the gutter by his mother as an infant. Tom is apprenticed at the Bounderby bank, and Sissy remains at the Gradgrind home to care for the younger children.

In the meantime, an impoverished "Hand"—Dickens's term for the lowest laborers in Coketown's factories—named Stephen Blackpool struggles with his love for Rachael, another poor factory worker. He is unable to marry her because he is already married to a horrible, drunken woman who disappears for months and even years at a time. Stephen visits Bounderby to ask about a divorce but learns that only the wealthy can obtain them. Outside Bounderby's home, he meets Mrs. Pegler, a strange old woman with an inexplicable devotion to Bounderby.

James Harthouse, a wealthy young sophisticate from London, arrives in Coketown to begin a political career as a disciple of Gradgrind, who is now a Member of Parliament. He immediately takes an interest in Louisa and decides to try to seduce her. With the unspoken aid of Mrs. Sparsit, a former aristocrat who has fallen on hard times and now works for Bounderby, he sets about trying to corrupt Louisa.

The Hands, exhorted by a crooked union spokesman named Slackbridge, try to form a union. Only Stephen refuses to join because he feels that a union strike would only increase tensions between employers and employees. He is cast out by the other

Hands and fired by Bounderby when he refuses to spy on them. Louisa, impressed with Stephen's integrity, visits him before he leaves Coketown and helps him with some money. Tom accompanies her and tells Stephen that if he waits outside the bank for several consecutive nights, help will come to him. Stephen does so, but no help arrives. Eventually he packs up and leaves Coketown, hoping to find agricultural work in the country. Not long after that, the bank is robbed, and the lone suspect is Stephen, the vanished Hand who was seen loitering outside the bank for several nights just before disappearing from the city.

Mrs. Sparsit witnesses Harthouse declaring his love for Louisa, and Louisa agrees to meet him in Coketown later that night. However, Louisa instead flees to her father's house, where she miserably confides to Gradgrind that her upbringing has left her married to a man she does not love, disconnected from her feelings, deeply unhappy, and possibly in love with Harthouse. She collapses to the floor, and Gradgrind, struck dumb with self-reproach, begins to realize the imperfections in his philosophy of rational self-interest.

Sissy, who loves Louisa deeply, visits Harthouse and convinces him to leave Coketown forever. Bounderby, furious that his wife has left him, redoubles his efforts to capture Stephen. When Stephen tries to return to clear his good name, he falls into a mining pit called Old Hell Shaft. Rachael and Louisa discover him, but he dies soon after an emotional farewell to Rachael. Gradgrind and Louisa realize that Tom is really responsible for robbing the bank, and they arrange to sneak him out of England with the help of the circus performers with whom Sissy spent her early childhood. They are nearly successful, but are stopped by Bitzer, a young man who went to Gradgrind's school and who embodies all the qualities of the detached rationalism that Gradgrind once espoused, but who now sees its limits. Sleary, the lisping circus proprietor, arranges for Tom to slip out of Bitzer's grasp, and the young robber escapes from England after all.

Mrs. Sparsit, anxious to help Bounderby find the robbers, drags Mrs. Pegler—a known associate of Stephen Blackpool—in to see Bounderby, thinking Mrs. Pegler is a potential witness. Bounderby recoils, and it is revealed that Mrs. Pegler is really his loving mother, whom he has forbidden to visit him: Bounderby is not a self-made man after all. Angrily, Bounderby fires Mrs. Sparsit and sends her away to her hostile relatives. Five years later, he will die alone in the streets of Coketown. Gradgrind gives up his philosophy of fact and devotes his political power to helping the poor. Tom realizes the error of his ways but dies without ever seeing his family again. While Sissy marries and has a large and loving family, Louisa never again marries and never has children. Nevertheless, Louisa is loved by Sissy's family and learns at last how to feel sympathy for her fellow human beings.

CHARACTER LIST

Thomas Gradgrind A wealthy, retired merchant in Coketown,
England; he later becomes a Member of Parliament.
Mr. Gradgrind espouses a philosophy of rationalism,
self-interest, and cold, hard fact. He describes himself
as an "eminently practical" man, and he tries to raise
his children—Louisa, Tom, Jane, Adam Smith, and
Malthus—to be equally practical by forbidding the
development of their imaginations and emotions.

Louisa Gradgrind's daughter, later Bounderby's wife.
Confused by her coldhearted upbringing, Louisa feels
disconnected from her emotions and alienated from
other people. While she vaguely recognizes that her
father's system of education has deprived her
childhood of all joy, Louisa cannot actively invoke her
emotions or connect with others. Thus she marries
Bounderby to please her father, even though she does
not love her husband. Indeed, the only person she loves
completely is her brother Tom.

Thomas Gradgrind, Jr. Gradgrind's eldest son and an apprentice
at Bounderby's bank, who is generally called Tom.
Tom reacts to his strict upbringing by becoming a
dissipated, hedonistic, hypocritical young man.
Although he appreciates his sister's affection, Tom
cannot return it entirely—he loves money and
gambling even more than he loves Louisa. These vices
lead him to rob Bounderby's bank and implicate
Stephen as the robbery's prime suspect.

Josiah Bounderby Gradgrind's friend and later Louisa's husband.
Bounderby claims to be a self-made man and boastfully
describes being abandoned by his mother as a young
boy. From his childhood poverty he has risen to
become a banker and factory owner in Coketown,
known by everyone for his wealth and power. His true

7

CHARACTER LIST

upbringing, by caring and devoted parents, indicates that his social mobility is a hoax and calls into question the whole notion of social mobility in nineteenth-century England.

Cecelia Jupe The daughter of a clown in Sleary's circus. Sissy is taken in by Gradgrind when her father disappears. Sissy serves as a foil, or contrast, to Louisa: while Sissy is imaginative and compassionate, Louisa is rational and, for the most part, unfeeling. Sissy embodies the Victorian femininity that counterbalances mechanization and industry. Through Sissy's interaction with her, Louisa is able to explore her more sensitive, feminine sides.

Mrs. Sparsit Bounderby's housekeeper, who goes to live at the bank apartments when Bounderby marries Louisa. Once a member of the aristocratic elite, Mrs. Sparsit fell on hard times after the collapse of her marriage. A selfish, manipulative, dishonest woman, Mrs. Sparsit cherishes secret hopes of ruining Bounderby's marriage so that she can marry him herself. Mrs. Sparsit's aristocratic background is emphasized by the narrator's frequent allusions to her "Roman" and "Coriolanian" appearance.

Stephen Blackpool A Hand in Bounderby's factory. Stephen loves Rachael but is unable to marry her because he is already married, albeit to a horrible, drunken woman. A man of great honesty, compassion, and integrity, Stephen maintains his moral ideals even when he is shunned by his fellow workers and fired by Bounderby. Stephen's values are similar to those endorsed by the narrator.

Rachael A simple, honest Hand who loves Stephen Blackpool. To Stephen, she represents domestic happiness and moral purity.

James Harthouse A sophisticated and manipulative young London gentleman who comes to Coketown to enter politics as a disciple of Gradgrind, simply because he thinks it might alleviate his boredom. In his constant search for a new form of amusement, Harthouse quickly becomes attracted to Louisa and resolves to seduce her.

Mr. Sleary The lisping proprietor of the circus where Sissy's father was an entertainer. Later, Mr. Sleary hides Tom Gradgrind and helps him flee the country. Mr. Sleary and his troop of entertainers value laughter and fantasy whereas Mr. Gradgrind values rationality and fact.

Bitzer Bitzer is one of the successes produced by Gradgrind's rationalistic system of education. Initially a bully at Gradgrind's school, Bitzer later becomes an employee and a spy at Bounderby's bank. An uncharacteristically pale character and unrelenting disciple of fact, Bitzer almost stops Tom from fleeing after it is discovered that Tom is the true bank robber.

Mr. McChoakumchild The unpleasant teacher at Gradgrind's school. As his name suggests, McChoakumchild is not overly fond of children, and stifles or chokes their imaginations and feelings.

Mrs. Pegler Bounderby's mother, unbeknownst as such to all except herself and Bounderby. Mrs. Pegler makes an annual visit to Coketown in order to admire her son's prosperity from a safe distance. Mrs. Pegler's appearance uncovers the hoax that her son Bounderby has been attesting throughout the story, which is that he is a self-made man who was abandoned as a child.

Mrs. Gradgrind Gradgrind's whiny, anemic wife, who constantly tells her children to study their "ologies" and complains that she'll "never hear the end" of any complaint. Although Mrs. Gradgrind does not share her husband's interest in facts, she lacks the energy and the imagination to oppose his system of education.

Slackbridge The crooked orator who convinces the Hands to unionize and turns them against Stephen Blackpool when he refuses to join the union.

Jane Gradgrind Gradgrind's younger daughter; Louisa and Tom's sister. Because Sissy largely raises her, Jane is a happier little girl than her sister, Louisa.

ANALYSIS OF MAJOR CHARACTERS

THOMAS GRADGRIND

Thomas Gradgrind is the first character we meet in *Hard Times,* and one of the central figures through whom Dickens weaves a web of intricately connected plotlines and characters. Dickens introduces us to this character with a description of his most central feature: his mechanized, monotone attitude and appearance. The opening scene in the novel describes Mr. Gradgrind's speech to a group of young students, and it is appropriate that Gradgrind physically embodies the dry, hard facts that he crams into his students' heads. The narrator calls attention to Gradgrind's "square coat, square legs, square shoulders," all of which suggest Gradgrind's unrelenting rigidity.

In the first few chapters of the novel, Mr. Gradgrind expounds his philosophy of calculating, rational self-interest. He believes that human nature can be governed by completely rational rules, and he is "ready to weigh and measure any parcel of human nature, and tell you what it comes to." This philosophy has brought Mr. Gradgrind much financial and social success. He has made his fortune as a hardware merchant, a trade that, appropriately, deals in hard, material reality. Later, he becomes a Member of Parliament, a position that allows him to indulge his interest in tabulating data about the people of England. Although he is not a factory owner, Mr. Gradgrind evinces the spirit of the Industrial Revolution insofar as he treats people like machines that can be reduced to a number of scientific principles.

While the narrator's tone toward him is initially mocking and ironic, Gradgrind undergoes a significant change in the course of the novel, thereby earning the narrator's sympathy. When Louisa confesses that she feels something important is missing in her life and that she is desperately unhappy with her marriage, Gradgrind begins to realize that his system of education may not be perfect. This intuition is confirmed when he learns that Tom has robbed Bounderby's bank. Faced with these failures of his system, Gradgrind admits, "The ground on which I stand has ceased to be solid under my feet."

His children's problems teach him to feel love and sorrow, and Gradgrind becomes a wiser and humbler man, ultimately "making his facts and figures subservient to Faith, Hope and Charity."

LOUISA GRADGRIND

Although Louisa is the novel's principal female character, she is distinctive from the novel's other women, particularly her foils, Sissy and Rachael. While these other two embody the Victorian ideal of femininity—sensitivity, compassion, and gentleness—Louisa's education has prevented her from developing such traits. Instead, Louisa is silent, cold, and seemingly unfeeling. However, Dickens may not be implying that Louisa is really unfeeling, but rather that she simply does not know how to recognize and express her emotions. For instance, when her father tries to convince her that it would be rational for her to marry Bounderby, Louisa looks out of the window at the factory chimneys and observes: "There seems to be nothing there but languid and monotonous smoke. Yet when the night comes, Fire bursts out." Unable to convey the tumultuous feelings that lie beneath her own languid and monotonous exterior, Louisa can only state a fact about her surroundings. Yet this fact, by analogy, also describes the emotions repressed within her.

Even though she does not conform to the Victorian ideals of femininity, Louisa does her best to be a model daughter, wife, and sister. Her decision to return to her father's house rather than elope with Harthouse demonstrates that while she may be unfeeling, she does not lack virtue. Indeed, Louisa, though unemotional, still has the ability to recognize goodness and distinguish between right and wrong, even when it does not fall within the strict rubric of her father's teachings. While at first Louisa lacks the ability to understand and function within the gray matter of emotions, she can at least recognize that they exist and are more powerful than her father or Bounderby believe, even without any factual basis. Moreover, under Sissy's guidance, Louisa shows great promise in learning to express her feelings. Similarly, through her acquaintance with Rachael and Stephen, Louisa learns to respond charitably to suffering and to not view suffering simply as a temporary state that is easily overcome by effort, as her father and Bounderby do.

JOSIAH BOUNDERBY

Although he is Mr. Gradgrind's best friend, Josiah Bounderby is more interested in money and power than in facts. Indeed, he is himself a fiction, or a fraud. Bounderby's inflated sense of pride is illustrated by his oft-repeated declaration, "I am Josiah Bounderby of Coketown." This statement generally prefaces the story of Bounderby's childhood poverty and suffering, a story designed to impress its listeners with a sense of the young Josiah Bounderby's determination and self-discipline. However, Dickens explodes the myth of the self-made man when Bounderby's mother, Mrs. Pegler, reveals that her son had a decent, loving childhood and a good education, and that he was not abandoned, after all.

Bounderby's attitude represents the social changes created by industrialization and capitalism. Whereas birth or bloodline formerly determined the social hierarchy, in an industrialized, capitalist society, wealth determines who holds the most power. Thus, Bounderby takes great delight in the fact that Mrs. Sparsit, an aristocrat who has fallen on hard times, has become his servant, while his own ambition has enabled him to rise from humble beginnings to become the wealthy owner of a factory and a bank. However, in depicting Bounderby, the capitalist, as a coarse, vain, self-interested hypocrite, Dickens implies that Bounderby uses his wealth and power irresponsibly, contributing to the muddled relations between rich and poor, especially in his treatment of Stephen after the Hands cast Stephen out to form a union.

STEPHEN BLACKPOOL

Stephen Blackpool is introduced after we have met the Gradgrind family and Bounderby, and Blackpool provides a stark contrast to these earlier characters. One of the Hands in Bounderby's factory, Stephen lives a life of drudgery and poverty. In spite of the hardships of his daily toil, Stephen strives to maintain his honesty, integrity, faith, and compassion.

Stephen is an important character not only because his poverty and virtue contrast with Bounderby's wealth and self-interest, but also because he finds himself in the midst of a labor dispute that illustrates the strained relations between rich and poor. Stephen is the only Hand who refuses to join a workers' union: he believes that striking is not the best way to improve relations between factory owners and employees, and he also wants to earn an honest living. As a result, he is cast out of the workers' group. However, he also refuses to spy on his fellow workers for Bounderby, who consequently sends him away. Both groups, rich and poor, respond in the same self-interested, backstabbing way. As Rachael explains, Stephen ends up with the "masters against him on one hand, the men against him on the other, he only wantin' to work hard in peace, and do what he felt right." Through Stephen, Dickens suggests that industrialization threatens to compromise both the employee's and employer's moral integrity, thereby creating a social muddle to which there is no easy solution.

Through his efforts to resist the moral corruption on all sides, Stephen becomes a martyr, or Christ figure, ultimately dying for Tom's crime. When he falls into a mine shaft on his way back to Coketown to clear his name of the charge of robbing Bounderby's bank, Stephen comforts himself by gazing at a particularly bright star that seems to shine on him in his "pain and trouble." This star not only represents the ideals of virtue for which Stephen strives, but also the happiness and tranquility that is lacking in his troubled life. Moreover, his ability to find comfort in the star illustrates the importance of imagination, which enables him to escape the cold, hard facts of his miserable existence.

THEMES, MOTIFS & SYMBOLS

THEMES

Themes are the fundamental and often universal ideas explored in a literary work.

THE MECHANIZATION OF HUMAN BEINGS

Hard Times suggests that nineteenth-century England's overzealous adoption of industrialization threatens to turn human beings into machines by thwarting the development of their emotions and imaginations. This suggestion comes forth largely through the actions of Gradgrind and his follower, Bounderby: as the former educates the young children of his family and his school in the ways of fact, the latter treats the workers in his factory as emotionless objects that are easily exploited for his own self-interest. In Chapter 5 of the first book, the narrator draws a parallel between the factory Hands and the Gradgrind children—both lead monotonous, uniform existences, untouched by pleasure. Consequently, their fantasies and feelings are dulled, and they become almost mechanical themselves.

The mechanizing effects of industrialization are compounded by Mr. Gradgrind's philosophy of rational self-interest. Mr. Gradgrind believes that human nature can be measured, quantified, and governed entirely by rational rules. Indeed, his school attempts to turn children into little machines that behave according to such rules. Dickens's primary goal in *Hard Times* is to illustrate the dangers of allowing humans to become like machines, suggesting that without compassion and imagination, life would be unbearable. Indeed, Louisa feels precisely this suffering when she returns to her father's house and tells him that something has been missing in her life, so much so that she finds herself in an unhappy marriage and may be in love with someone else. While she does not actually behave in a dishonorable way, since she stops her interaction with Harthouse before she has a socially ruinous affair with him, Louisa realizes that her life is unbearable and that she must do something drastic for her own survival. Appealing to her father with the utmost honesty, Louisa is able to make him realize and admit that his philosophies on life and methods of child rearing are to blame for Louisa's detachment from others.

THE OPPOSITION BETWEEN FACT AND FANCY

While Mr. Gradgrind insists that his children should always stick to the facts, *Hard Times* not only suggests that fancy is as important as fact, but it continually calls into question the difference between fact and fancy. Dickens suggests that what constitutes so-called fact is a matter of perspective or opinion. For example, Bounderby believes that factory employees are lazy good-for-nothings who expect to be fed "from a golden spoon." The Hands, in contrast, see themselves as hardworking and as unfairly exploited by their employers. These sets of facts cannot be reconciled because they depend upon perspective. While Bounderby declares that "[w]hat is called Taste is only another name for Fact," Dickens implies that fact is a question of taste or personal belief. As a novelist, Dickens is naturally interested in illustrating that fiction cannot be excluded from a fact-filled, mechanical society. Gradgrind's children, however, grow up in an environment where all flights of fancy are discouraged, and they end up with serious social dysfunctions as a result. Tom becomes a hedonist who has little regard for others, while Louisa remains unable to connect with others even though she has the desire to do so. On the other hand, Sissy, who grew up with the circus, constantly indulges in the fancy forbidden to the Gradgrinds, and lovingly raises Louisa and Tom's sister in a way more complete than the upbringing of either of the older siblings. Just as fiction cannot be excluded from fact, fact is also necessary for a balanced life. If Gradgrind had not adopted her, Sissy would have no guidance, and her future might be precarious. As a result, the youngest Gradgrind daughter, raised both by the factual Gradgrind and the fanciful Sissy, represents the best of both worlds.

THE IMPORTANCE OF FEMININITY

During the Victorian era, women were commonly associated with supposedly feminine traits like compassion, moral purity, and emotional sensitivity. *Hard Times* suggests that because they possess these traits, women can counteract the mechanizing effects of industrialization. For instance, when Stephen feels depressed about the monotony of his life as a factory worker, Rachael's gentle fortitude inspires him to keep going. He sums up her virtues by referring to her as his guiding angel. Similarly, Sissy introduces love into the Gradgrind household, ultimately teaching Louisa how to recognize her emotions. Indeed, Dickens suggests that Mr. Gradgrind's philosophy of self-interest and calculating rationality has prevented Louisa from developing her natural feminine traits. Perhaps Mrs. Gradgrind's inability to exercise her femininity allows Gradgrind to overemphasize the importance of fact in the rearing of his children. On his part, Bounderby ensures that his rigidity will remain untouched since he marries the cold, emotionless product of Mr. and Mrs. Gradgrind's marriage. Through the various female characters in the novel, Dickens suggests that feminine compassion is necessary to restore social harmony.

MOTIFS

Motifs are recurring structures, contrasts, or literary devices that can help to develop and inform the text's major themes.

BOUNDERBY'S CHILDHOOD

Bounderby frequently reminds us that he is "Josiah Bounderby of Coketown." This emphatic phrase usually follows a description of his childhood poverty: he claims to have been born in a ditch and abandoned by his mother; raised by an alcoholic grandmother; and forced to support himself by his own labor. From these ignominious beginnings, he has become the wealthy owner of both a factory and a bank. Thus, Bounderby represents the possibility of social mobility, embodying the belief that any individual should be able overcome all obstacles to success—including poverty and lack of education—through hard work. Indeed, Bounderby often recites the story of his childhood in order to suggest that his Hands are impoverished because they lack his ambition and self-discipline. However, "Josiah Bounderby of Coketown" is ultimately a fraud. His mother, Mrs. Pegler, reveals that he was raised by parents who were loving, albeit poor, and who saved their money to make sure he received a good education. By exposing Bounderby's real origins, Dickens calls into question the myth of social mobility. In other words, he suggests that perhaps the Hands cannot overcome poverty through sheer determination alone, but only through the charity and compassion of wealthier individuals.

MOTIFS

CLOCKS AND TIME

Dickens contrasts mechanical or man-made time with natural time, or the passing of the seasons. In both Coketown and the Gradgrind household, time is mechanized—in other words, it is relentless, structured, regular, and monotonous. As the narrator explains, "Time went on in Coketown like its own machine." The mechanization of time is also embodied in the "deadly statistical clock" in Mr. Gradgrind's study, which measures the passing of each minute and hour. However, the novel itself is structured through natural time. For instance, the titles of its three books—"Sowing," "Reaping," and "Garnering"—allude to agricultural labor and to the processes of planting and harvesting in accordance with the changes of the seasons. Similarly, the narrator notes that the seasons change even in Coketown's "wilderness of smoke and brick." These seasonal changes constitute "the only stand that ever was made against its direful uniformity." By contrasting mechanical time with natural time, Dickens illustrates the great extent to which industrialization has mechanized human existence. While the changing seasons provide variety in terms of scenery and agricultural labor, mechanized time marches forward with incessant regularity.

MISMATCHED MARRIAGES

There are many unequal and unhappy marriages in *Hard Times*, including those of Mr. and Mrs. Gradgrind, Stephen Blackpool and his unnamed drunken wife, and most pertinently, the Bounderbys. Louisa agrees to marry Mr. Bounderby because her father convinces her that doing so would be a rational decision. He even cites statistics to show that the great difference in their ages need not prevent their mutual happiness. However, Louisa's consequent misery as Bounderby's wife suggests that love, rather than either reason or convenience, must be the foundation of a happy marriage.

SYMBOLS

Symbols are objects, characters, figures, or colors used to represent abstract ideas or concepts.

STAIRCASE

When Mrs. Sparsit notices that Louisa and Harthouse are spending a lot of time together, she imagines that Louisa is running down a long staircase into a "dark pit of shame and ruin at the bottom."

This imaginary staircase represents her belief that Louisa is going to elope with Harthouse and consequently ruin her reputation forever. Mrs. Sparsit has long resented Bounderby's marriage to the young Louisa, as she hoped to marry him herself; so she is very pleased by Louisa's apparent indiscretion. Through the staircase, Dickens reveals the manipulative and censorious side of Mrs. Sparsit's character. He also suggests that Mrs. Sparsit's self-interest causes her to misinterpret the situation. Rather than ending up in a pit of shame by having an affair with Harthouse, Louisa actually returns home to her father.

PEGASUS

Mr. Sleary's circus entertainers stay at an inn called the Pegasus Arms. Inside this inn is a "theatrical" pegasus, a model of a flying horse with "golden stars stuck on all over him." The pegasus represents a world of fantasy and beauty from which the young Gradgrind children are excluded. While Mr. Gradgrind informs the pupils at his school that wallpaper with horses on it is unrealistic simply because horses do not in fact live on walls, the circus folk live in a world in which horses dance the polka and flying horses can be imagined, even if they do not, in fact, exist. The very name of the inn reveals the contrast between the imaginative and joyful world of the circus and Mr. Gradgrind's belief in the importance of fact.

SMOKE SERPENTS

At a literal level, the streams of smoke that fill the skies above Coketown are the effects of industrialization. However, these smoke serpents also represent the moral blindness of factory owners like Bounderby. Because he is so concerned with making as much profit as he possibly can, Bounderby interprets the serpents of smoke as a positive sign that the factories are producing goods and profit. Thus, he not only fails to see the smoke as a form of unhealthy pollution, but he also fails to recognize his own abuse of the Hands in his factories. The smoke becomes a moral smoke screen that prevents him from noticing his workers' miserable poverty. Through its associations with evil, the word "serpents" evokes the moral obscurity that the smoke creates.

SYMBOLS

FIRE

When Louisa is first introduced, in Chapter 3 of Book the First, the narrator explains that inside her is a "fire with nothing to burn, a starved imagination keeping life in itself somehow." This description suggests that although Louisa seems coldly rational, she has not succumbed entirely to her father's prohibition against wondering and imagining. Her inner fire symbolizes the warmth created by her secret fancies in her otherwise lonely, mechanized existence. Consequently, it is significant that Louisa often gazes into the fireplace when she is alone, as if she sees things in the flames that others—like her rigid father and brother—cannot see. However, there is another kind of inner fire in *Hard Times*—the fires that keep the factories running, providing heat and power for the machines. Fire is thus both a destructive and a life-giving force. Even Louisa's inner fire, her imaginative tendencies, eventually becomes destructive: her repressed emotions eventually begin to burn "within her like an unwholesome fire." Through this symbol, Dickens evokes the importance of imagination as a force that can counteract the mechanization of human nature.

SYMBOLS

Summary & Analysis

Book the First: Sowing: Chapters 1–4

Now what I want is Facts. (See QUOTATIONS, p. 49)

Summary — Chapter 1: The One Thing Needful

In an empty schoolroom, a dark-eyed, rigid man emphatically expresses to the schoolmaster and another adult his desire for children to be taught facts, saying that "nothing else will ever be of any service to them."

Summary — Chapter 2: Murdering the Innocents

In the industrial city of Coketown, a place dominated by grim factories and oppressed by coils of black smoke, the dark-eyed, rigid man—Thomas Gradgrind—has established a school. He has hired a teacher, Mr. McChoakumchild, whom he hopes will instill in the students nothing but cold, hard facts. Visiting the school, Gradgrind tests a pair of students by asking them to define a horse. Sissy Jupe, the daughter of a horse-riding circus entertainer, is unable to answer, but a pale young man called Bitzer gives a cut-and-dried definition that pleases Gradgrind.

Summary — Chapter 3: A Loophole

While walking back to his home, appropriately named Stone Lodge, Gradgrind catches his two eldest children spying on the circus through a peephole in the fence. Having raised his children according to his philosophy of fact and having permitted them no imaginative entertainment, Gradgrind becomes furious. He drags the young Tom and sixteen-year-old Louisa home. Louisa admits that curiosity drew her to the circus and tries to defend her brother by saying she dragged him there, but all Gradgrind can do is ask angrily what Mr. Bounderby would say.

Summary — Chapter 4: Mr. Bounderby

This same Mr. Bounderby—a wealthy, boastful industrialist who owns factories and a bank—is at that very moment in the drawing room at Stone Lodge, pontificating to the pallid and lethargic Mrs. Gradgrind about his poverty-stricken childhood. Bounderby never fails to talk at length about this subject. He reminds Mrs. Gradgrind that he was born in a ditch, abandoned by his mother, and raised by a cruel, alcoholic grandmother. At this point, Gradgrind enters and tells Bounderby about his children's misbehavior. Mrs. Gradgrind scolds the children halfheartedly, admonishing them to "go and be somethingological." Bounderby theorizes that Sissy Jupe, the circus entertainer's daughter who attends Gradgrind's school, may have led the young Gradgrinds astray. Gradgrind agrees, and they set out to inform Sissy's father that Sissy is no longer welcome at the school. Bounderby demands a kiss from Louisa before they leave.

ANALYSIS — BOOK THE FIRST: SOWING: CHAPTERS 1–4

Dickens was concerned with the miserable lives of the poor and working classes in the England of his day, and *Hard Times* is one of several of his novels that addresses these social problems directly. *Hard Times* is not Dickens's most subtle novel, and most of its moral themes are explicitly articulated through extremely sharp, exaggerated characterization, and through the narrator's frequent interjection of his own opinions and sentiments. For instance, in the opening section of the book, a simple contrast emerges between Mr. Gradgrind's philosophy of fact and Sissy Jupe's frequent indulgence in romantic, imaginative fancy. While Gradgrind's philosophy includes the idea that people should only act according to their own best interests, which they can calculate through rational principles, the actions of the simple, loving Sissy are inspired by her feelings, usually of compassion toward others. The philosophy of fact is continually shown to be at the heart of the problems of the poor—the smokestacks, factory machines, and clouds of black smog are all associated with fact—while fancy is held up as the route to charity and love between fellow men. Philosophically, this contrast is a drastic and obvious oversimplification. Clearly, a commitment to factual accuracy does not lead directly to selfishness, and a commitment to imagination does not signify a commitment to social equality. But for the purposes of *Hard Times,* these contrasting ideas serve as a kind of shorthand for the states of mind that enable certain kinds of action. Cold rationalism divorced from sentiment and feeling can lead to insensitivity about human suffering, and imagination can enhance one's sense of sympathy.

Gradgrind's philosophy of fact is intimately related to the Industrial Revolution, a cause of the mechanization of human nature. Dickens suggests that when humans are forced to perform the same monotonous tasks repeatedly, in a drab, incessantly noisy, and smoky environment, they become like the machines with which they work—unfeeling and not enlivened by fancy. The connection between Gradgrind's philosophy of fact and the social effects of the Industrial Revolution is made explicit by two details in the first section of the novel. First, the narrator reports that when Gradgrind finds his children at the circus, "Tom gave himself up to be taken home like a machine." By dulling Tom's feelings and his sense of free will, his education has rendered his thoughts and actions mechanical. The second detail illustrating the connection between Gradgrind's philosophy and the process of industrialization is the choice of names for Gradgrind's two younger sons, Adam Smith and Malthus. These children play no role in the plot, but their names are relevant to the novel's themes. Adam Smith (1723–1790) was a Scottish economist who produced the theory that the economy is controlled by an "invisible hand," and that employers and workers do not control the fluctuations of supply and demand. Malthus (1766–1834) was an economist who argued that poverty is a result of overpopulation and that the poor must have smaller families in order to improve the general standard of living in society. Both of these writers addressed the poverty of mind and body that accompanies industrialization. Through these two names, Dickens suggests that the philosophy of fact to which Gradgrind subscribes and the deleterious social effects of the Industrial Revolution are inextricably related.

This first section serves mainly to introduce the contrast between fact and fancy and to establish the allegiances of the main characters. From the very first paragraph, Mr. Gradgrind is established as the leading disciple of fact, but he is also shown to be a loving, if deluded, father. The real villain of the novel is Mr. Bounderby, who seems to share Mr. Gradgrind's love of fact but has no difficulty lying about himself, as later events show. Sissy is clearly on the side of feeling and fancy, as are all the circus performers. Louisa seems torn between the world of her upbringing and a deep inner desire to experience imagination and feeling—a desire that she lacks the vocabulary even to name. Her unhappy status, lost between the worlds of fact and fancy, combined with Bounderby's obvious attraction toward her, serves as the catalyst for the principal conflict in the novel.

SUMMARY & ANALYSIS

BOOK THE FIRST: SOWING: CHAPTERS 5–8

SUMMARY — CHAPTER 5: THE KEY-NOTE

On their way to find Sissy's father, Gradgrind and Bounderby walk through the dark, smoky streets of Coketown, passing a number of identically shaped buildings made from identical dirty red bricks. Soon they meet Sissy Jupe herself, who is being chased by the bullying Bitzer. Sissy, a dutiful and loving daughter, has been out buying oils for her father's aches and pains. The two men follow her back to the dwelling place of the circus performers.

SUMMARY — CHAPTER 6: SLEARY'S HORSEMANSHIP

Sissy stops at an inn called the Pegasus Arms, where Bounderby and Gradgrind are introduced to the lisping circus master, Mr. Sleary. Sleary informs Gradgrind that, unbeknownst to Sissy, her father has lost his ability as a performer and has abandoned her in shame. Gradgrind decides to take Sissy into his home and raise her according to his philosophy of fact. Sissy agrees to the arrangement, principally because she believes her father will come back for her—an idea that Bounderby and Gradgrind find fanciful and ridiculous. A strange assortment of circus folk gathers to wish Sissy well in her new home. She is sorry to leave them, because these entertainers have been like a family to Sissy during her childhood.

SUMMARY — CHAPTER 7: MRS. SPARSIT

The next day, Bounderby discusses Louisa with his housekeeper, Mrs. Sparsit, who is connected to the prominent aristocratic Powler family. After falling on hard times, the aristocratic Mrs. Sparsit has accepted employment with Mr. Bounderby, but she constantly reminds him of her family connections. Bounderby worries that the fanciful Sissy will be a bad influence on Louisa, whom he already regards as his future wife. Gradgrind informs Sissy that she may continue to attend his school and that she will care for Mrs. Gradgrind in her free time.

SUMMARY — CHAPTER 8: NEVER WONDER

Later that same day, Louisa talks with her brother about her father's plan to apprentice Tom at Mr. Bounderby's bank. Both Louisa and Tom are depressed by the colorless monotony of life at Stone Lodge, but Louisa, attempting to cheer up Tom, reminds him of her affection for him. She seems to feel that something is missing from her life, but when she wonders what it might be, Mrs. Gradgrind warns Louisa never to wonder—wondering contradicts the philosophy of fact, and it also makes Mrs. Gradgrind wish she had never been cursed with a family.

ANALYSIS — BOOK THE FIRST: SOWING: CHAPTERS 5–8

In Dickens's novels, characters' names often reveal details about their personalities. For instance, Mr. Gradgrind's name evokes the monotonous grind of his children's lives, as well as the grinding of the factory machines. Similarly, the title of each chapter in *Hard Times* can be helpful in interpreting the movement of the plot. For example, the first chapter is titled "The One Thing Necessary," and in this chapter we learn that Mr. Gradgrind believes the one thing necessary for a fulfilling existence is fact. The meaning of the title of Chapter 5, "The Key-note," is not so immediately obvious. However, its meaning is clarified at the beginning of Chapter 8, when the narrator declares, "Let us strike the key-note again before pursuing the tune." He then describes how, as a child, Louisa was inclined to wonder about the world around her, to ask questions, and to imagine. Not surprisingly, her father quickly suppressed this inclination, telling Louisa that she must "never wonder." In Chapter 5, the narrator also draws our attention to the need for wonder and imagination when he compares the Gradgrind children to factory workers. He explains that both the children and the workers "have Fancy in them demanding to be brought into healthy existence." From these passages, we can conclude that the conflict between fact and fancy is the "key-note," or the key theme, that the narrator will continue to bring up throughout the novel. Fancy, the narrator implies, is at least as important as fact in a balanced, fulfilling existence. Chapters 5 through 8 thus serve to reinforce the relationship between fact and fancy.

In this section, the circus entertainers are the most obvious representatives of fancy, and Gradgrind accordingly finds them rather distasteful. The entertainers possess the ability to transform the colorless, humdrum world into a place of magic and excitement simply by using their imaginations. This transformation is illustrated by Kidderminster, a gruff young boy who plays the role of Cupid in the circus. In real life, Kidderminster is cheeky, loud, and temperamental, but in the circus ring he is adorably sweet and wins the specta-tors' hearts. Through fancy, the circus entertainers not only find happiness themselves, but also bring pleasure to others.

In Chapter 8, Dickens draws attention to another mode of fancy that brings pleasure to others: fiction, and in particular, novels. The narrator relates that, much to Mr. Gradgrind's dismay, factory workers flock to the Coketown library "to read mere fables about men and women, more or less like themselves, and about children, more or less like their own." The workers are drawn to these stories because they stimulate their imaginations, causing them to wonder about "human nature, human passions, human hopes and fears, the struggles, the triumphs and defeats . . . of common men and women." Novels provide a much-needed escape from the drab, mechanical factories in which these workers spend most of their days. In describing the workers' reading habits, Dickens draws attention to the fact that his own readers are in fact reading a novel about, more or less, ordinary men and women. Thus, he presents his novels as a way to counteract the dehumanizing effects of the Indus-trial Revolution. Significantly, the Coketown workers read what is known as realism, or fiction that attempts to represent real life accu-rately, and which often describes the lives of common people rather than those of kings, queens, and other aristocrats. In his focus on the common man and the social conditions of Victorian England, Dick-ens himself is a realist writer. In this passage, he reminds us that even realism is a form of fancy and that even realist novels can both teach us about real life and awaken our imaginations. The realist novel, he suggests, combines fact and fancy. In Victorian England, the novel was often considered a dangerous genre precisely because it was accessible to the working and middle classes. Many people feared that novels would corrupt the minds of these readers by making them too fanciful and even by giving them immoral ideas. By sug-gesting that realist novels can both teach and entertain, Dickens defends his novel against these charges.

SUMMARY & ANALYSIS

BOOK THE FIRST: SOWING: CHAPTERS 9–12

> *. . . not all the calculators of the National debt can tell*
> *me the capacity for good or evil, for love or hatred,*
> *for patriotism or discontent, for the decomposition of*
> *virtue into vice. . . .*   (See QUOTATIONS, p. 50)

SUMMARY — CHAPTER 9: SISSY'S PROGRESS
Sissy Jupe does very poorly at the school because she is simply unable to adopt the cold, hard devotion to fact that is demanded of her. Instead, she continues to cling to what Mr. Gradgrind thinks of as ridiculous, fanciful notions, such as the idea that her father will come back for her. One day, Louisa convinces Sissy secretly to talk about life with her father. Louisa, raised to never feel strong emotion, finds herself very moved by Sissy's deep feelings. During the conversation with Sissy, Tom frequently reminds Louisa to watch out for Bounderby, in case he should catch her "wondering" about Sissy's past.

SUMMARY — CHAPTER 10: STEPHEN BLACKPOOL
One night, in the most hardworking, grimy district of Coketown, a simple and brutally poor man named Stephen Blackpool goes home from his job as a power loom operator in Mr. Bounderby's factory. Stephen is a Hand, one of the lowest menial laborers in Coketown. He talks briefly in the street to Rachael, the pure, honest woman he loves, then goes home, where he is stunned to find his wayward, immoral, and generally absent wife lying in his bed. In order to soothe the misery of poverty, his wife has become an alcoholic, and although Stephen wishes to divorce her, he nevertheless pities her.

SUMMARY — CHAPTER 11: NO WAY OUT
Disturbed by his wife's sudden reappearance, Stephen visits Mr. Bounderby the next day to ask humbly if he has any legal recourse and any possibility of obtaining a divorce. Arrogantly, and with many references to his own impoverished childhood, Bounderby explains that only the wealthy can obtain divorces and that Stephen would be better off accepting his miserable situation.

SUMMARY — CHAPTER 12: THE OLD WOMAN

Outside Bounderby's house, Stephen meets a strange old woman who has traveled into the city from the country. She tells Stephen that every year she saves enough money to make the long journey into Coketown for a single day, just long enough to catch a glimpse of Mr. Bounderby. She fears that Bounderby will not come out of his house that day and says that seeing Stephen just after he saw Bounderby must satisfy her for this year. The old woman follows him to Bounderby's grim factory and inexplicably praises its beauty. After work is over for the day, Stephen wanders the streets, trying to avoid going home to his drunken wife. As he wanders, Stephen imagines the pleasant, happy home he could share with Rachael if only he were free to remarry.

ANALYSIS — BOOK THE FIRST: SOWING: CHAPTERS 9–12

With the introduction of Stephen Blackpool, the novel delves into the world of the Hands, the working-class, horribly impoverished denizens of Coketown whom Dickens uses to represent the plight of the poor. Stephen, with his simple honesty and love for the angelic Rachael, is shown to be a good character despite his horrible marriage. He immediately contrasts with the blustery, self-obsessed Bounderby, a difference hammered home when Stephen visits his employer to ask about the possibility of divorcing his wife. Having heard that there is a law permitting divorce under certain circumstances, Stephen inquires into the details of this law. However, Bounderby makes it clear that there are no laws to help Stephen—all laws are made by the rich, for the rich. Bounderby callously tells Stephen that, as a poor man, he has no recourse but to accept his lot. Furthermore, Bounderby reminds Stephen that "[t]here's a sanctity in the relation" of marriage that "must be kept up." Although he shows no pity for Stephen's misery, these words later come back to haunt Bounderby when his own marriage becomes troubled.

On top of his utter lack of pity, Bounderby then accuses Stephen of wanting to eat turtle soup with a gold spoon. This accusation results from Bounderby's belief that all Hands are improvident, dishonest cretins who simply want to get ahead, when in reality Bounderby, who very well could eat turtle soup with a gold spoon, is the only character guilty of fitting that description. His belief that Hands are lazy good-for-nothings is part of his rhetoric of the self-made man. As he constantly reminds us, he managed to rise from his

humble beginnings to become the wealthy owner of factories and a bank. If the Hands were not so lazy, he implies, surely they could do the same.

While Stephen and Rachael are the only Hands who become fully developed characters in the course of the novel, Dickens provides many generalized views of the Hands and their working conditions. Like the novel itself, these impressions are structured through the contrast between fact and fancy. For instance, at the beginning of Chapter 11, the narrator describes the awakening of the Coketown factories: "The Fairy palaces burst into illumination before pale morning showed the monstrous serpents of smoke trailing themselves over Coketown." The fairy palaces are, in fact, simply the factories bursting with light as the fires are lit inside them. While Dickens suggests that fancy can make even Coketown beautiful and magical, the image is ironic because these palaces house the poorest segment of society and are filled with noise, grime, and smoke. While the description of Coketown does not specify the horrors of the Hands' working conditions, it does create a general impression of filth and noise.

Dickens has been criticized for not developing his working-class characters fully, or not depicting them in as much detail as his middle-class characters. For instance, when the narrator describes the Hands at work, he merely states: "So many hundred Hands in the Mill; so many hundred horse Steam Power." The term "Hands" itself depersonalizes the workers by referring to them by the part of their body that performs their tasks in the factories. Much of *Hard Times* is devoted to pointing out how the middle classes ignore the poor. Perhaps, then, Dickens is calling for a more sympathetic and insightful examination of the working and living conditions of poor people in Victorian England. The narrator implies as much when he declares that "not all the calculators of the National Debt can tell me the capacity for good or evil . . . in one of these its quiet servants." The narrator thus points out how little is known about the poor and how little interest society shows in their thoughts, feelings, and problems. *Hard Times* does not fully answer the question of how the poor live, but instead tries to impel us to start asking this question for ourselves.

BOOK THE FIRST: SOWING: CHAPTERS 13–16

Thou art an Angel. Bless thee, bless thee!
(See QUOTATIONS, p. 51)

SUMMARY — CHAPTER 13: RACHAEL

When Stephen finally returns to his room, he is shocked to find Rachael sitting next to his bedridden wife, tending to what appears to be a serious illness. Rachael tells Stephen to go to sleep in the chair. Stephen falls asleep, but wakes up just in time to see his wife about to swallow a lethal amount of one of her medicines. Stephen is unable to act, but Rachael awakens suddenly and seizes the bottle from the sick woman, thereby preventing her death. Ashamed of his inability to bring himself to stop his wife's attempted suicide, Stephen looks upon Rachael as an angel.

SUMMARY — CHAPTER 14: THE GREAT MANUFACTURER

Time passes, moving relentlessly like the machinery of a factory. Mr. Gradgrind tells Sissy that she is hopeless at the school but that she may continue to live at Stone Lodge and care for Mrs. Gradgrind. Gradgrind has become a Member of Parliament, and he spends much of his time in London. Tom, now a dissipated, hedonistic young man, tells Louisa that her father intends to arrange a marriage between her and Mr. Bounderby, with whom Tom, as an apprentice in the bank, now lives. He encourages Louisa to accept, so that they might live together again, and tells her that she is his best defense against Mr. Bounderby's authority.

SUMMARY — CHAPTER 15: FATHER AND DAUGHTER

When her father raises the prospect of marriage, Louisa seems puzzled—she does not understand why she is being asked to love the fifty-year-old Bounderby. Although she is sure that she does not love him, she agrees to marry him, asking, "What does it matter?" Louisa realizes that she does not, in fact, know how to love, but she is anxious to please her father by marrying his friend.

SUMMARY — CHAPTER 16: HUSBAND AND WIFE

Bounderby tentatively mentions his marriage to Mrs. Sparsit, suggesting that she should take a position keeping the apartments at Bounderby's bank after he and Louisa get married. Mrs. Sparsit evidently disapproves of the marriage, stating ambiguously that she hopes Bounderby is as happy as he deserves to be. Bounderby attempts to show his affection for his bride-to-be by showering her with jewels and fine clothes, but she remains impassive. At the last moment, however, Louisa clings to Tom in fear, feeling that she is taking a drastic and perhaps irrevocable step. Nevertheless, Bounderby and Louisa are united in matrimony, and they set out on a honeymoon trip to Lyons, as Bounderby wants to observe the operations of some factories there.

ANALYSIS — BOOK THE FIRST: SOWING: CHAPTERS 13–16
The question of how women, marriage, and the home fit into an industrialized, mechanized society now comes to the forefront. During the Victorian Era, the home was widely regarded as a place of relaxation and pleasure and as an escape from the moral corruption of the business world and from the grinding monotony of factory life—in short, as a refuge from the working world. In *Hard Times,* however, the distinction between home and workplace begins to dissolve. For instance, the Gradgrind household is almost as mechanized as a factory. Similarly, when Stephen's drunken wife suddenly returns, his home no longer provides a refuge from the misery of his factory work, so he resorts to wandering the streets rather than returning home after work. In both of these instances, the home fails to serve as a refuge from the working world.

The homes presented in *Hard Times* derive their tone from whatever female inhabits them. For instance, Gradgrind's wife, who is too complacent to argue with her husband over his mechanistic ways, allows him to determine the fact-heavy tone of the home. Stephen's wife, the lascivious drunk, makes their home a wanton den to which Stephen is reluctant to return. In contrast to Stephen's wife, Rachael embodies the qualities that make home a happy place—she is compassionate, honest, sensitive, morally pure, and generous. She represents the Victorian ideal of femininity. Because of these qualities, Stephen frequently refers to her as his angel. Through her own virtues, Rachael inspires him to maintain his personal integrity, and when she cares for his ailing wife, Rachael lightens the tone of the previously dismal residence.

The other women in the novel also play an important role in the quality of the home. Mrs. Sparsit, in contrast to Rachael, is proud and manipulative—because she is motivated solely by self-interest, she has no desire to waste her time bringing happiness to others. Although Louisa loves her brother Tom, her education prevents her from developing the qualities that Rachael embodies. Only Sissy shares Rachael's compassionate, loving nature. For most of the nineteenth century, a woman's job was to care for the home and children, and to make home a happy, relaxing place. By depicting women who not only deviate from the Victorian ideal of femininity, but also fail in their jobs as homemakers, Dickens suggests that industrialization threatens to dissolve the boundaries between workplace and home, without the stabilizing force of femininity.

This section of *Hard Times* depicts two marriages that are unhappy because the couples are badly matched. Stephen's hard-working integrity contrasts sharply with his wife's dissolute drunkenness, but despite realizing that his marriage was a mistake, Stephen has no alternative but to put up with his wife. Louisa and Bounderby's marriage threatens to be unhappy because they are separated not only by an age difference of about thirty years, but by their inability to communicate with each other. While Louisa does not know how to recognize and express her feelings, Bounderby is only interested in his own feelings and does not really care about hers. Through these mismatched couples, Dickens suggests that a happy marriage must be founded upon mutual love and respect. Mr. Gradgrind, however, tries to reduce marriage, and indeed love itself, to a question of logic. When Louisa asks his advice about whether she should marry Bounderby, her father tells her "to consider this question as you have been accustomed to consider every other question, simply as one of Fact." Gradgrind believes that the question of whether marrying Bounderby would be the best course of action for Louisa can be decided by looking at empirical evidence. Thus, he cites some statistics about the relative ages of husbands and wives to show that a young wife and an older husband can have a happy marriage. Based on these statistics, and on the fact that she has received no other proposals of marriage, Gradgrind calculates that it would be in Louisa's best interest to marry Bounderby. The fact that Bounderby takes Louisa to observe the factories in Lyon for their honeymoon further emphasizes the lack of romance in their relationship, which is purely a marriage of convenience and practicality. Through Louisa's marriage, Dickens again depicts the mechanization of family life. By negating the importance of love, Gradgrind's philosophy of fact turns humans into machines and the home into a veritable factory.

BOOK THE SECOND: REAPING: CHAPTERS 1–4

Coketown lay shrouded in a haze of its own . . .
suggestive of itself, though not a brick of it could be
seen.   (See QUOTATIONS, p. 52)

SUMMARY — CHAPTER 1: EFFECTS IN THE BANK

On one of Coketown's rare sunny days, Mrs. Sparsit sits in her apartment in the bank and talks to Bitzer, a former pupil at Gradgrind's school, and now a porter at the bank. The two are discussing the young Tom Gradgrind, who, although he still works at the bank, has become a "dissipated, extravagant idler." A very well-dressed young gentleman interrupts their conversation by knocking at the door. The stranger explains that he has come to Coketown to enter politics as a disciple of Gradgrind. His suave manner and genteel appearance please Mrs. Sparsit, and she attempts to flatter him. The young man inquires about Louisa Bounderby, of whom he has heard intimidating reports: he imagines that she must be middle-aged, quick-witted, and formidable. When Mrs. Sparsit assures him that Mrs. Bounderby is simply a lovely young woman, he seems very relieved and interested.

SUMMARY & ANALYSIS

SUMMARY — CHAPTER 2: MR. JAMES HARTHOUSE

We learn that the strange visitor's name is James Harthouse and that he is a disingenuous, wealthy young man who is only interested in Gradgrind's politics because he hopes they will alleviate his pervasive boredom. He does not really share Gradgrind's philosophy of fact, but he is prepared to pretend that he does in order to pass the time. Harthouse goes to dinner at Bounderby's, where he is very intrigued by Louisa.

SUMMARY — CHAPTER 3: THE WHELP

After dinner, Harthouse takes the caddish young Tom—who is highly impressed with his new acquaintance's amoral worldliness—back to his apartment. Harthouse plies Tom with wine and tobacco and then coaxes the story of Louisa's marriage out of him. The drunken Tom claims that Louisa only married Bounderby for Tom's sake, so that she could use Bounderby's money to help her brother with his own financial difficulties. Once Harthouse learns that Louisa does not love her husband, he privately resolves to seduce her.

SUMMARY — CHAPTER 4: MEN AND BROTHERS

Elsewhere in Coketown, the factory Hands, who have decided to unionize in an attempt to improve their wretched conditions, hold a meeting. An inflammatory orator named Slackbridge gives an impassioned speech about the necessity of unionizing and of showing their sense of fellowship. The only Hand who remains unconvinced is Stephen Blackpool. Stephen says he does not believe that the union will do any good because it will only aggravate the already tense relationship between employers and workers. After he voices this opinion, he is cast out of the meeting. The other Hands—his longtime friends and companions—agree to shun him as a sign of their solidarity. Stephen asks them only to allow him to continue working. He endures four days of ostracism before Bitzer summons him to Bounderby's house.

ANALYSIS — BOOK THE SECOND: REAPING: CHAPTERS 1–4

At the beginning of Book the Second, Dickens displays his knack for using characterization to articulate his moral themes with the character of Mrs. Sparsit. If Stephen represents the poor and Bounderby and Gradgrind represent the wealthy middle class, Mrs. Sparsit and Harthouse are satires of the aristocracy. Dependent on Bounderby for her well-being, Mrs. Sparsit is adept at manipulating her circumstances around her belief that she is a great lady wronged by others. Much as Bounderby takes pride in his humble origins, Mrs. Sparsit frequently brings up the fact that she descends from one of the best families in the kingdom. Dickens often satirizes her by describing her control over her features, claiming that she makes her aristocratic Roman nose "more Roman" in a moment of outrage. In this section, she uses Bitzer to gain useful information about the other bank employees. She is clearly spying, but pretends to be too ladylike to want to hear their names. Nevertheless, she manages to ascertain that Bitzer believes young Tom to be a horrible employee.

The two main events in this section are the arrival of James Harthouse, with his menacing amorality and his desire to seduce Louisa, and the union meeting, with Stephen's expulsion from the company of his fellow Hands. Harthouse, with his worldly cynicism and sophisticated boredom, is immediately presented as a foil to the more provincial characters in Coketown. He is neither committed to the philosophy of fact nor capable of any fancy; rather, he is simply looking out of his aristocratic haze for something to pass the time. He is perfectly equipped to capitalize on Louisa's inner confusion and capable of awakening her feelings without caring about the result. Harthouse is a stereotypical aristocratic dandy—he is not motivated by the desire for wealth or power, but rather by boredom and the desire for some new form of entertainment. Louisa presents a special source of interest because he has never met anyone like her before and cannot fully understand her.

The union meeting takes us deeper into the world of the Hands and allows Dickens to satirize the everyday, agitating spokesman with the harshly drawn caricature of Slackbridge. The narrator informs us that Slackbridge differs from the other Hands in that he is "not so honest, he [is] not so manly, he [is] not so good-humored." His primary intention is apparently to stir up the workers' feelings until they are in an impassioned frenzy against their employers. Dickens's own feelings about labor unions, and about any attempt to right wrongs through hostility and conflict, are expressed through Stephen's views. Stephen immediately recognizes that Slackbridge does not care so much about creating unity among workers as he does about creating tension between employers and employees. This tension, Stephen believes, will do nothing to aid the workers in their desire for better working conditions and pay. Thus, Stephen asks only to be allowed to make his living in peace: "I mak' no complaints . . . o' being outcasten and overlooken, fro this time forrard, but I hope I shall be let to work." Stephen is unwilling to sacrifice his belief in what is right, even if he will be made a pariah. With his hardworking integrity, Stephen represents a very sentimental and idealized portrait of a poor worker, which Dickens wields to arouse our sympathy. Through the contrast between Slackbridge and Stephen, however, Dickens suggests that the working class contains both good and bad individuals, just like the rest of society.

BOOK THE SECOND: REAPING: CHAPTERS 5–8

. . . we are awlus wrong, and never had'n no reason in us sin ever we were born. (See QUOTATIONS, p. 53)

SUMMARY — CHAPTER 5: MEN AND MASTERS

Bounderby attempts to cajole Stephen into telling him what went on at the union meeting, but Stephen refuses to be used as a spy. He says that Slackbridge is no more to blame for the desire of the workers to unionize than a clock is to blame for the passing of time, but he repeats his belief that the union will do no good. When he refuses to spy on the other Hands, Bounderby angrily dismisses him from the factory. Because his fellow Hands have ostracized him, Stephen will have to leave Coketown in search of work.

SUMMARY — CHAPTER 6: FADING AWAY

Outside Bounderby's, Stephen encounters Rachael with the old woman he met once before, who introduces herself as Mrs. Pegler. Stephen takes the pair back to his room for tea, telling Rachael the news of his dismissal. In spite of Stephen's misfortune, they pass an enjoyable evening and are surprised by the appearance of Louisa and Tom at Stephen's door. Louisa was impressed with Stephen's refusal to help her husband break up the union, and she offers him money to help him on his way. Deeply touched, Stephen agrees to accept only two pounds, which he promises to pay back. Tom summons Stephen outside and makes him another offer of help. Tom tells Stephen to wait outside the bank late at night for the next few nights, and if all goes well, someone will appear with assistance. Stephen spends the next few days preparing to leave Coketown, and he waits outside the bank each evening, following Tom's instructions. He notices several people observing his loitering, including Mrs. Sparsit and Bitzer, but no one comes to offer him help. Finally, one morning, Stephen walks by Rachael's house one last time, then sets out down the road out of Coketown, the trees arching over him, his own heart aching for the loving heart of Rachael that he is leaving behind.

SUMMARY — CHAPTER 7: GUNPOWDER

As James Harthouse begins to enjoy some political success, he also begins to plan his seduction of Louisa. He and Louisa spend a lot of time together at Bounderby's country estate near Coketown, and through their private conversations he learns how to manipulate the emotions that Louisa herself does not know she has. Realizing that her brother is the only person for whom she truly cares, Harthouse uses his influence over Tom to make him act more kindly to Louisa—and he makes sure she knows who is responsible.

SUMMARY — CHAPTER 8: EXPLOSION

One morning, Bounderby charges in upon Harthouse and Louisa, announcing that the bank has been robbed of roughly 150 pounds. The only suspect is Stephen Blackpool, who was seen loitering outside the bank late at night, shortly before fleeing from Coketown. Mrs. Sparsit, whose nerves have been shocked by the event, temporarily moves in with the Bounderbys, where she begins to spend more and more time with Mr. Bounderby, and insists upon referring to Louisa as "Miss Gradgrind." Knowing that her brother is deeply in debt, Louisa suspects Tom of stealing the money. She confronts him about it one night, and he protests his innocence. However, as soon as she leaves his room, he buries his face in his pillow and begins to sob guiltily.

ANALYSIS — BOOK THE SECOND: REAPING: CHAPTERS 5–8

Thus far, *Hard Times* has consisted of two seemingly separate plot strands—the first involving Louisa and Bounderby's loveless marriage, and the second describing Stephen's ostracism from his fellow workers. In this section, however, these plots begin to coverge. This interweaving of the previously separate plot strands is illustrated by Stephen and Louisa's meeting in Chapter 6, a meeting that brings Louisa into contact with a person of the working class for the first time in her life. This meeting illustrates that Louisa is not entirely without compassion or feeling, and it serves to further awaken her latent emotions. Previously, Louisa had known the Hands only as "[s]omething to be worked so much and paid so much," but in going to Stephen's room, she sees for the first time the suffering that these individuals experience.

The meeting at Stephen's room is also important because it sets the stage for the bank robbery. While Louisa shows her ability to feel compassion, Tom reveals his self-interested, manipulative side when he tells Stephen that help may come to him if he waits outside the bank for several consecutive nights, since Tom is the person who robs Bounderby and frames Stephen. The weaving together of the two plots signifies that the narrative is approaching its climax, the moment when the conflict erupts.

This section of the novel also reveals changes in Tom and Louisa's relationship. Ever since Tom asked Louisa to marry Bounderby for his sake, he has been growing increasingly distant from his sister. While he formerly confided in her and treated her affectionately, Tom now becomes sulky, refusing to answer her questions regarding his knowledge of the bank robbery. Indeed, Louisa is beset by problems on all sides. Not only must she contend with Tom's sulky silence and his requests for money, but she is also prey to Mr. Harthouse's advances. Meanwhile, Bounderby remains oblivious to her precarious situation, as he is concerned only with the bank robbery. Again, Louisa's problems point toward the approaching climax of the novel.

The reappearance of the mysterious Mrs. Pegler in Chapter 6 illustrates the important role that seemingly minor characters play in Dickens's novels. Characters such as Bitzer, Mr. Sleary, and Mrs. Pegler serve to draw together the many divergent plot strands, thereby moving the narrative forward. With Mrs. Pegler's second appearance, we begin to realize that she must be somehow important to the plot. While Dickens keeps us in suspense about who she is and why she is important, he does provide some significant clues. For instance, when Stephen asks her if she has any children, Mrs. Pegler does not say that her son is dead, but instead replies, "I have lost him." Furthermore, when Mrs. Pegler believes that Bounderby is about to enter Stephen's room, she becomes extremely agitated and looks for a means to escape. From these details, and from the fact that she journeys to Coketown each year simply to catch a glimpse of him, we can infer that Mrs. Pegler is in some way connected to Bounderby.

BOOK THE SECOND: REAPING:
CHAPTERS 9–12

SUMMARY — CHAPTER 9: HEARING THE LAST OF IT

Mrs. Sparsit continues to lurk around the Bounderby estate, flattering Bounderby's pride and worming her way into his good graces. She also observes shrewdly that Louisa spends a great deal of time with James Harthouse. It is not long, however, before this new pattern is interrupted: Louisa receives a letter from Stone Lodge, telling her that her mother is dying. Louisa rushes to her mother's side and sees that her younger sister, Jane, who is being raised primarily by Sissy, seems happier and more fulfilled than Louisa felt as a child. Before her death, Mrs. Gradgrind calls Louisa to her, explaining that she feels like she has missed or forgotten something and that she wants to write a letter to Mr. Gradgrind asking him to find out what it is. After a whining farewell, Mrs. Gradgrind dies.

SUMMARY — CHAPTER 10: MRS. SPARSIT'S STAIRCASE

Even after Mrs. Sparsit leaves the Bounderbys, she continues to visit very frequently. Thinking about Louisa's burgeoning relationship with Mr. Harthouse, Mrs. Sparsit begins to imagine that Louisa is on a giant staircase leading into a black abyss. She pictures Louisa running downward and downward, and she takes great pleasure in imagining what will happen when she reaches the bottom and falls into this abyss.

SUMMARY — CHAPTER 11: LOWER AND LOWER

One day, Mrs. Sparsit discovers that Tom has been sent to the train station in Coketown to wait for Harthouse and that Louisa is at the country estate, all alone. Suspecting a ruse and ignoring a driving rain, Mrs. Sparsit hurries to the country, where she heads into the forest and discovers Louisa and Harthouse in an intimate conversation. Harthouse professes his love for Louisa and states his desire to become her lover. Louisa agrees to meet him in town later that night but urges him to leave immediately. He does so, and Louisa at once sets out for Coketown. Scrambling to follow her, Mrs. Sparsit gleefully imagines Louisa tumbling off the precipice at the bottom of her imaginary staircase. However, she loses track of Louisa before Louisa reaches her ultimate destination.

SUMMARY — CHAPTER 12: DOWN

Contrary to Mrs. Sparsit's expectations, Louisa does not go to meet James Harthouse but instead goes to Stone Lodge, where she rushes into her father's study, drenched to the bone and extremely upset. She confesses to her father that she bitterly regrets her childhood and says that the way he brought her up exclusively on facts, without ever letting her feel or imagine anything, has ruined her. She claims that she is married to a man she despises and that she may be in love with Harthouse. Consequently, she is thoroughly miserable and does not know how to rectify the situation. Gradgrind is shocked and consumed with sudden self-reproach. Sobbing, Louisa collapses to the floor.

ANALYSIS — BOOK THE SECOND: REAPING: CHAPTERS 9–12

After a great deal of buildup, this section constitutes the climax of the story, in which the primary conflicts erupt into the open. Louisa's collapse gives Dickens a chance to show the damaging consequences of Gradgrind's method of raising his children. Deprived of any connection with her own feelings, Louisa is empty and baffled. When she suddenly discovers her own emotions, the pain of the discovery overwhelms her. Gradgrind, formerly the most potent believer in the philosophy of fact, also sees how his philosophy has warped his daughter, and he begins to reform.

Significantly, Mrs. Gradgrind also realizes before her death that something, although she does not know what, has been missing from her family's life, something that she can recognize in Sissy Jupe. Even though Mrs. Gradgrind is unable to communicate this revelation to her husband, he learns through Louisa's collapse that his philosophy has deprived his family of the happiness that only imagination and love can create.

Mrs. Sparsit's imaginary staircase symbolizes the standards of social conduct during the Victorian era. If a woman spent time alone with a man who was not her relative, her behavior was considered morally suspect, or a sign of her possible mental, if not physical, unchasteness. If Louisa had indeed eloped with Harthouse, her reputation would have been ruined irreparably—as it is, her character has merely fallen under Mrs. Sparsit's suspicion. Mrs. Sparsit's mental staircase also emphasizes the manipulative and even vicious side of her own personality. While pretending to be a model of virtue, Mrs. Sparsit secretly takes pleasure in the idea of Louisa's fall. Structurally, this section marks the moment in the novel in which the villains stand most triumphantly over the good characters: Harthouse and Mrs. Sparsit have destroyed Louisa emotionally; Bounderby and Tom, who is, of course, the real bank robber, have ruined Stephen's good name; and Gradgrind is devastated by Louisa's collapse.

The third section of the novel affords the good characters an opportunity to improve these miserable conditions, largely with the aid of the purest, most innocent, and most fanciful character of them all: the once-maligned Sissy Jupe. In general, the structure of *Hard Times* is extremely simple, but it is also important to the development of the action. The novel is divided into three sections, "Sowing," "Reaping," and "Garnering"—agricultural titles that are ironic alongside the industrial focus of the novel. In the first section, the seeds are planted for the rest of the novel—Sissy comes to live with the Gradgrinds, Louisa is married to Bounderby, and Tom is apprenticed at the bank. In the second section, the characters reap the results of those seeds—Louisa's collapse, Tom's robbery, and Stephen's exile. In the third section, whose title, "Garnering," literally means picking up the pieces of the harvest that were missed, the characters attempt to restore equilibrium to their lives, and they face their futures with new emotional resources at their disposal.

The titles of the sections, however, refer not only to the harvesting of events, but also to the harvesting of ideas. In the first chapter of *Hard Times,* Gradgrind declares his intention to "plant" only facts in his children's minds, and to "root out everything else," such as feelings and fancies. This metaphor returns to haunt him when, just before her collapse, Louisa points to the place where her heart should be and asks her father, "[W]hat have you done with the garden that should have bloomed once, in this great wilderness here?" Louisa implies that by concentrating all his efforts on planting facts in his children's minds, Gradgrind has neglected to plant any sentiments in their hearts, leaving her emotionally barren.

BOOK THE THIRD: GARNERING: CHAPTERS 1–4

SUMMARY — CHAPTER 1: ANOTHER THING NEEDFUL
In her bed at Stone Lodge, Louisa recuperates from her trauma. Her father remorsefully pledges his support but acknowledges that he does not really know how to help her because he himself has never learned "the wisdom of the Heart." Sissy lovingly vows to help Louisa learn how to feel and how to find happiness.

SUMMARY — CHAPTER 2: VERY RIDICULOUS
The day after Louisa's arrival, Sissy takes it upon herself to visit James Harthouse, who has been in a nervous state since Louisa's failure to appear at their tryst in Coketown. Sissy tells Harthouse that he will never see Louisa again and that he must leave Coketown and swear never to return. Baffled and feeling very ridiculous, Harthouse is able to resist neither Sissy's simple, persuasive honesty nor her beauty; he grudgingly agrees to leave Coketown forever.

SUMMARY — CHAPTER 3: VERY DECIDED
At the same time, Mrs. Sparsit, now stricken with a bad cold caught from her drenching in the rain, tells Bounderby what she witnessed between Louisa and Harthouse. Bounderby furiously drags Mrs. Sparsit to Stone Lodge, where he confronts Gradgrind about Louisa's perceived infidelity. Gradgrind tells Bounderby that he fears he has made a mistake in Louisa's upbringing, and he asks Bounderby to allow Louisa to remain at Stone Lodge on an extended visit while she tries to recover. He reminds Bounderby that as Louisa's husband, he should try to do what is best for her. Bounderby, enraged, threatens to send back all of Louisa's property, effectively abandoning her and placing her back in her father's hands if she is not home by noon the next day. Gradgrind does not budge, and Louisa remains at Stone Lodge. Bounderby makes good on his threat and resumes his life as a bachelor.

SUMMARY — CHAPTER 4: LOST
Bounderby diverts his rage into the continuing efforts to find Stephen Blackpool. Slackbridge gives a speech blaming Stephen for the robbery, and the Hands are roused to track him down. One day, Louisa is paid a visit by Bounderby, her brother, and a sobbing

Rachael, who protests that Stephen will return to clear his good name. Although she is loath to suspect Louisa of deceit, Rachael fears that Louisa's previous offer of money was merely a cover for her plan to frame Stephen for the robbery. Rachael has sent Stephen two letters explaining the charges against him, and she claims that he will return to Coketown in one or two days. But a week passes, and still he does not return. His continued absence only increases suspicion against him.

ANALYSIS — BOOK THE THIRD: GARNERING: CHAPTERS 1–4
At the beginning of Book the Third, Louisa and Mr. Gradgrind begin a process of emotional healing and discovery. The title of Chapter 1, "Another Thing Needful," echoes the title of the first chapter of Book the First, "The One Thing Needful," revealing that Gradgrind has realized that fact alone cannot sustain a happy and fulfilling existence. However, the healing process is very slow. Because Louisa and her father are so accustomed to living their lives according to the philosophy of fact, learning how to change their mode of thinking is difficult at this point. Thus, Mr. Gradgrind declares to Louisa: "The ground on which I stand has ceased to be solid under my feet." Although he no longer believes that fact alone is necessary, he does not know exactly what else is needed to make Louisa happy. Recognizing that he is not a fit teacher for his daughter, Gradgrind hopes that Sissy will be able to help her. While Louisa fears that Sissy must hate her for her former coldness, Sissy is understanding and forgiving, as usual. Together with Louisa's loving younger sister Jane, Sissy undertakes to restore happiness to Louisa's life.

The meeting between Harthouse and Sissy indicates the importance of a character who has remained in the background for much of the novel. Through this meeting we are reminded of the values that Sissy represents—compassion, forgiveness, and joy. The narrator establishes a contrast between these values and the sophisticated Harthouse's self-centered manipulation of other people. Indeed, the narrator relates that Sissy's good-natured reproach touches Harthouse "in the cavity where his heart should have been." In suggesting that Harthouse has no heart, the narrator suggests that he has not been motivated by evil intentions but rather by a lack of good intentions—Harthouse is amoral rather than immoral. Harthouse himself acknowledges that he had "no evil intentions" toward Louisa but merely "glided from one step to another" without realizing the emotional havoc that his seduction might cause.

Like Bounderby, Tom, and Mrs. Sparsit, Harthouse is motivated only by his own interest and does not consider how his actions might impact other people. Through these characters, Dickens again illustrates the moral dangers of a society that values fact more than feeling. Ultimately, Harthouse, the worldly cynic, is completely overpowered by Sissy Jupe, the loving innocent; he is easily sent away from Coketown, never to threaten Louisa again.

In this section of the novel, Dickens returns to the issue of the Hands' unionization, again suggesting that unionization does not in fact unite individuals, but divides them, turning one person against another. While Slackbridge repeatedly addresses the other Hands as "fellow-countrymen," "fellow-brothers," "fellow-workmen," and "fellow-citizens," he ironically encourages them to exclude Stephen from their fellowship. Rather than supporting their fellow worker in his time of need, they disown him. Rachael sums up Stephen's predicament when she declares despairingly: "The masters against him on one hand, the men against him on the other, he only wantin' to work hard in peace, and do what he felt right. Can a man have no soul of his own, no mind of his own?" In his unfailing integrity and his desire for peace and harmony, Stephen becomes a martyr. He suffers not only for what he believes in but also for another person's crime.

BOOK THE THIRD: GARNERING: CHAPTERS 5–9

SUMMARY — CHAPTER 5: FOUND

Sissy visits Rachael every night as they wait for news of Stephen. One night, as they are walking past Bounderby's house, they see Mrs. Sparsit dragging Mrs. Pegler into the house. Mrs. Sparsit tells Bounderby she has found the old woman, who was seen in Blackpool's apartment before the robbery, and has brought him the possible accessory to the crime for questioning. But far from being pleased, Bounderby is furious: Mrs. Pegler is his mother, and as their encounter falls out, it becomes clear to the assembled company that she did not abandon him in the gutter, as he had claimed. Rather, she raised, educated, and loved him. He abandoned her, refusing to allow her to visit him now that he has become wealthy and successful. The myth of Bounderby, the self-made man, is exploded, and he refuses to offer an explanation for his former lies about his past.

SUMMARY — CHAPTER 6: THE STARLIGHT

Stephen still fails to appear. One morning, Sissy takes Rachael for a walk in the country to restore her strength, and they discover Stephen's hat. Rachael instantly fears that he has been murdered, but, after walking on a little farther, they discover that he has fallen down an old mining pit called Old Hell Shaft and is still clinging to life. The women seek help, and a large crowd assembles around the pit. A rescue team manages to lift Stephen out, and a doctor attends to his injuries. Nonetheless, after bidding a loving farewell to Rachael and telling Louisa to have Gradgrind ask Tom for the information that will clear his name, Stephen dies.

SUMMARY — CHAPTER 7: WHELP-HUNTING

When the crowd disperses, Tom is missing. Back at Stone Lodge, Gradgrind and Louisa feel that their fears are confirmed: Tom robbed the bank. Louisa reveals that Sissy encouraged Tom to seek refuge with Mr. Sleary's circus, currently camped near Liverpool. From there, Tom might leave England on one of the many boats sailing for South America or the Indies. Relieved that Tom might escape prison, Sissy, Louisa, and Gradgrind set out in two separate coaches for Mr. Sleary's circus, hoping to send Tom safely out of the country. Louisa and Sissy travel all night and reunite with Sleary, who tells Sissy that Tom is safe. Gradgrind arrives not long after. They are joined by the sullen Tom, who has been participating in the circus performance dressed up in blackface. They agree to send him up the coast to Liverpool, where he can book passage out of the country. Tom is rude to Louisa, blaming her for his predicament because she refused to finance his gambling habit, but she cries out that she forgives him and that she loves him still. Suddenly, the pale-faced Bitzer appears and says that Tom cannot leave, for he intends to take him back to Coketown and hand him over to the police.

SUMMARY — CHAPTER 8: PHILOSOPHICAL

With the assistance of some of Sleary's circus people, Bitzer takes Tom to arrange rail passage back to Coketown. However, Sleary double-crosses Bitzer with a trick involving madly barking dogs and dancing horses, which enables Tom to escape aboard ship after all. The next morning, Tom's family learns that he is safely away from England. Sleary has one more surprise in store: he confides to Gradgrind that Merrylegs, Sissy's father's dog, has unexpectedly returned alone to the circus, a sure sign that her father is dead.

SUMMARY — CHAPTER 9: FINAL

In the aftermath of the incident with Mrs. Pegler, Bounderby fires Mrs. Sparsit and sends her away to live with her unpleasant relative, Lady Scadgers. Looking proudly at his portrait, Mr. Bounderby does not guess that he will die from a fit in the streets of Coketown in a mere five years' time. The narrator reveals that in that future, Gradgrind will cease serving fact and will instead devote his skills and money to faith, hope, and charity. He will also publish writings exonerating the name of Stephen Blackpool. Furthermore, the narrator discloses that Louisa will never marry again. Tom will soon repent of his hostility toward his sister, and he will die abroad longing for a last look at Louisa's face. Rachael will go on working and continue in her sweetness and good faith, and Sissy will have a large and happy family. Louisa will be deeply loved by Sissy's children, through whom she will vicariously experience the joy and wonder of childhood. And Louisa will always strive to understand and improve the lives of her fellow human beings.

ANALYSIS — BOOK THE THIRD: GARNERING: CHAPTERS 5–9

In this section, everyone gets their just desserts. The narrator demonstrates his omniscience and his moral authority by assigning futures to the main characters according to each of their situations and merits. In other words, the characters who are clearly good are rewarded with happy endings, while those who are clearly bad end up miserable. Bounderby is exposed as a fraud with the revelation that his life story is a lie designed to cover up his wretched treatment of his kindly mother. Mrs. Sparsit is packed off to Lady Scadgers, having ruined her own chances with Bounderby through her excessive nosiness. Tom manages to escape but realizes the guilt of his awful behavior after it is too late to make amends with Louisa, and he dies, missing her terribly. Sissy, of course, ends up happy. The one exception to this general rule of poetic justice is the death of Stephen Blackpool. While Stephen seems to look forward to death as a release from his miserable existence, he leaves Rachael bereft and alone after he dies. Rachael's misery and Stephen's undeserved death are perhaps a part of Dickens's intent to rouse sympathy for the poor.

Unlike Bounderby and Sissy, some of the characters in *Hard Times* cannot be clearly labeled as either good or bad. The narrator assigns ambiguous futures to these characters—they are not simply rewarded, but neither are they simply punished. Of these ambiguous futures, Mr. Gradgrind's fate is perhaps the most ironic of all. At the beginning of the novel, he reviles the circus troupe and accuses it of corrupting his children. At the end, he is forced to depend on the troupe to save one of his children. After that, he behaves morally, devoting his political power to helping the poor, but is in turn reviled by the fact-obsessed politicians whose careers he helped to create.

Louisa is the most ambiguous character in the novel, and she faces an equally mixed fate: free of Bounderby and free of Harthouse, she is loved by Sissy's children, but she never has a family of her own. In wrapping up the plot, Dickens strays from his concern with social problems in favor of a focus on the inner lives of his characters. The book does not offer any resolution to the situation of the Hands beyond advocating love and fellowship among men, and the end of the novel is designed to let us know how each character will fare in the future, rather than how larger social issues will be addressed. At the heart of Dickens's writing, social protest and satire are almost always secondary to the more fundamental issues of character and story. *Hard Times* is remarkable among Dickens's fiction in that the focus on social ills is prominent throughout the novel, but in the end, Dickens's attention for his characters prevails.

IMPORTANT QUOTATIONS EXPLAINED

1. Now, what I want is Facts. Teach these boys and girls
    nothing but Facts. Facts alone are wanted in life. Plant
    nothing else, and root out everything else. You can
    only form the mind of reasoning animals upon Facts:
    nothing else will ever be of any service to them.

These are the novel's opening lines. Spoken by Mr. Gradgrind, they sum up his rationalist philosophy. In claiming that "nothing else will ever be of service" to his pupils, Gradgrind reveals his belief that facts are important because they enable individuals to further their own interests. However, Tom and Louisa's unhappy childhood soon calls into question their father's claim that "[f]acts alone are wanted in life." Ironically, while Gradgrind refers to the pupils in his school as "reasoning animals" and compares their minds to fertile soil in which facts can be sowed, he treats them like machines by depriving them of feeling and fantasy. His jarringly short sentences and monotonous repetition of the word "Fact" illustrate his own mechanical, unemotional character. Finally, it is significant that Gradgrind's call for facts opens a work of fiction. By drawing attention to the fact that we are reading fiction, Dickens suggests to us that facts alone cannot bring intellectual pleasure.

QUOTATIONS

2. It is known, to the force of a single pound weight, what the engine will do; but not all the calculators of the National debt can tell me the capacity for good or evil, for love or hatred, for patriotism or discontent, for the decomposition of virtue into vice, or the reverse, at any single moment in the soul of one of these quiet servants, with the composed faces and the regulated actions.

This passage, from Book the First, Chapter 11, provides insight into the narrator's beliefs and opinions. Dickens's omniscient narrator assumes the role of a moral guide, and his opinion tends to shape our own interpretations of the story. Here, we learn that the narrator disagrees with Gradgrind, believing instead that human nature cannot be reduced to a bundle of facts and scientific principles. The narrator invokes the mystery of the human mind, pointing out how little we actually know about what motivates the actions of our fellow beings. The "quiet servants" to whom the narrator refers are the factory Hands. In representing these people as an unknown quantity, the narrator counteracts Bounderby's stereotypes of the poor as lazy, greedy good-for-nothings. While he suggests that we need to understand these people better, the narrator also implies that this knowledge cannot be attained through calculation, measurement, and/or the accumulation of fact.

3.   Thou art an Angel. Bless thee, bless thee!

More a symbol than a fully developed character, Rachael is often referred to as an angel by Stephen. Like Sissy Jupe, whom she later befriends, Rachael represents the qualities necessary to counteract the dehumanizing, morally corrupting effects of industrialization. She is compassionate, honest, generous, and faithful to Stephen, even when everyone else shuns him and considers him a thief. As this remark illustrates, Rachael also draws out Stephen's good qualities, making him realize that joy can be found even in the moral darkness of Coketown. Rachael and Sissy are both socially marginal characters—the former is a Hand, and the latter is the daughter of a circus entertainer. Likewise, they are both relatively minor characters in the novel. Through their marginal status, Dickens implies that the self-serving rationalism that dominates Coketown threatens to exclude the morally pure people who are necessary to save society from complete corruption.

QUOTATIONS

4. Coketown lay shrouded in a haze of its own, which
    appeared impervious to the sun's rays. You only knew
    the town was there because you knew there could
    have been no such sulky blotch upon the prospect
    without a town. A blur of soot and smoke, now
    confusedly tending this way, now that way, now
    aspiring to the vault of Heaven, now murkily creeping
    along the earth, as the wind rose and fell, or changed
    its quarter: a dense formless jumble, with sheets of
    cross light in it, that showed nothing but masses of
    darkness—Coketown in the distance was suggestive of
    itself, though not a brick of it could be seen.

Like many other descriptions of Coketown, this passage, from Book
the Second, Chapter 1, emphasizes its somber smokiness. The
murky soot that fills the air represents the moral filth that permeates
the manufacturing town. Similarly, the sun's rays represent both the
physical and moral beauty that Coketown lacks. While the pollution from the factories makes Coketown literally a dark, dirty place
to live, the suffering of its poor and the cold self-interest of its rich
inhabitants render Coketown figuratively dark. In stating that
Coketown's appearance on the horizon is "suggestive of itself," the
narrator implies that Coketown is exactly what it appears to be. The
dark "sulky blotch" hides no secrets but simply represents what is,
on closer inspection, a dark, formless town. Built entirely of hard,
red brick, Coketown has no redeeming beauty or mystery—instead,
it embodies Mr. Gradgrind's predilection for unaccommodating
material reality.

5. Look how we live, an' wheer we live, an' in what
   numbers, an' by what chances, an' wi' what sameness;
   and look how the mills is awlus a-goin', and how they
   never works us no nigher to onny distant object-
   'ceptin awlus Death. Look how you considers of us,
   and writes of us, and talks of us, and goes up wi' your
   deputations to Secretaries o' State 'bout us, and how
   yo are awlus right, and how we are awlus wrong, and
   never had'n no reason in us sin ever we were born.
   Look how this ha' growen an' growen sir, bigger an'
   bigger, broader an' broader, harder an' harder, fro
   year to year, fro generation unto generation. Who can
   look on't sir, and fairly tell a man 'tis not a muddle?

Stephen Blackpool's speech to Bounderby, from Book the Second, Chapter 5, is one of the few glimpses that we receive into the lives of the Hands. His long sentences and repetition of words such as "an'" and "Look" mimic the monotony of the workers' lives. Similarly, Stephen's dialect illustrates his lack of education and contrasts with the proper English spoken by the middle-class characters and by the narrator. In spite of his lack of formal education, however, Stephen possesses greater insight about the relationship between employer and employee than does Bounderby. Stephen notes that "yo" (the factory owners and employers) and "us" (the Hands) are constantly opposed, but that the Hands stand no chance in the contest because the employers possess all the wealth and power. However, he does not blame the employers solely for the suffering of the poor, concluding instead that the situation is a "muddle" and that it is difficult to determine who is responsible for society's ills. Stephen also suggests that the monotony of factory labor seems futile to the Hands, who need to strive for some larger goal in order to make the endless round of production seem worthwhile. The "distant object" or larger goal that he mentions here is later symbolized by the bright star on which he gazes while trapped at the bottom of the mine shaft.

KEY FACTS

FULL TITLE
Hard Times for These Times

AUTHOR
Charles Dickens

TYPE OF WORK
Novel

GENRE
Victorian novel; realist novel; satire; dystopia

LANGUAGE
English

TIME AND PLACE WRITTEN
1854, London

DATE OF FIRST PUBLICATION
Published in serial installments in Dickens's magazine *Household Words* between April 1 and August 12, 1854

PUBLISHER
Charles Dickens

NARRATOR
The anonymous narrator serves as a moral authority. By making moral judgments about the characters, the narrator shapes our interpretations of the novel.

POINT OF VIEW
The narrator speaks in the third person and has a limited omniscience. He knows what is going on in all places and at all times, but he sometimes speculates about what the characters might be feeling and thinking, suggesting, at those times, that he does not actually know.

TONE
The narrator's tone varies drastically, but it is frequently ironic, mocking, and even satirical, especially when he describes Bounderby, Harthouse, and Mrs. Sparsit. When describing Stephen and Rachael, his tone is pathetic, evoking sympathy.

TENSE

The narrative is presented in the past tense; however, at the end, the narrator reveals what the future will bring to each of the main characters.

SETTING (TIME)

The middle of the nineteenth century

SETTING (PLACE)

Coketown, a manufacturing town in the south of England

PROTAGONIST

Louisa Gradgrind

MAJOR CONFLICT

Louisa Gradgrind struggles to reconcile the fact-driven self-interest of her upbringing with the warmth of feeling that she witnesses both in Sissy Jupe and developing within herself. As this attitude changes, Louisa is caught between allegiances to her family and loveless marriage and her desire to transcend the emotional and personal detachment of her past.

RISING ACTION

Sissy joins the Gradgrind household, and Louisa marries Mr. Bounderby unwillingly, only to satisfy her father's sense of what would be most rational for her.

CLIMAX

Mr. Harthouse joins Gradgrind's political disciples and attempts to seduce Louisa. Louisa, confused, leaves Bounderby and returns to her father's house, where she collapses.

FALLING ACTION

Sissy informs Harthouse that Louisa will never see him again, and Louisa attempts to amend her life by appealing to her father and offering assistance to the alleged perpetrator in Bounderby's bank robbery.

THEMES

The mechanization of human beings; the opposition between fact and fancy; the importance of femininity

MOTIFS

Bounderby's childhood; clocks and time; mismatched marriages

SYMBOLS

Staircase; pegasus; fire; smoke serpents

FORESHADOWING

Stephen's claim that factory Hands have only death to look forward to foreshadows his own death in the mine shaft. Bitzer's run-in with Mr. Gradgrind at the circus at the beginning of the novel, when he has been taunting Sissy, foreshadows his run-in with Mr. Gradgrind at the circus at the end of the novel, when Tom is fleeing the country.

Study Questions & Essay Topics

Study Questions

1. Hard Times *is a novel about the social condition of poverty, but very few of its major characters are actually poor and comparatively little time is spent with the poor characters. With that in mind, do you think the book does an effective job of shaping our view of poverty? Why or why not?*

It may be that Dickens chose to center his novel on the wealthy middle class rather than on the lower classes he sought to defend because he realized that most of his Victorian readers would come from the middle classes and that very few of his readers would come from the lower classes. By centering his book on characters with whom his readers could identify, he was better able to awaken their feelings for characters with whom they might otherwise be unable to identify—namely, the poor of Coketown and of England in general. In that sense, the book does its job. Of course, the contrary argument could also be made that the novel simply reinforces comfortable middle-class stereotypes about the noble poor, and it offers no real solution or possibility for change.

2. *Mrs. Sparsit is a fairly minor character in* Hard Times.
    *What themes does she illustrate? Why is she important in
    terms of plot development?*

Although Mrs. Sparsit is a relatively minor character, her pride
drives much of the action in the second half of the novel. Originally
from an aristocratic background, Mrs. Sparsit has fallen on hard
times, and she must work as Bounderby's housekeeper for a living.
Because she wants to marry Bounderby so that she can share his
wealth, Mrs. Sparsit secretly connives to destroy his marriage to
Louisa. Yet even while she panders to Bounderby, Mrs. Sparsit considers him an upstart "Noodle," and considers herself his superior
because of her aristocratic blood. Although she is a proud aristocrat, Mrs. Sparsit shares the calculating self-interest of capitalists
like Bounderby. Thus, Mrs. Sparsit illustrates the transition from a
social hierarchy in which aristocrats hold the power to one in which
the wealthy middle class holds the power. In her attempt to retain
her power within a new social order, Mrs. Sparsit simply ends up
looking ridiculous.

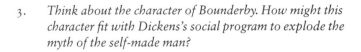

3. *Think about the character of Bounderby. How might this character fit with Dickens's social program to explode the myth of the self-made man?*

One defense of the new economic conditions created by the Industrial Revolution was its expansion of individual opportunity. The wealthy could justify the condition of the poor by pointing out that if the poor worked industriously, they could work their way into a fortune. Dickens implicitly mocks that idea by presenting one such supposed self-made man as a blundering braggart. By exposing Bounderby as a fraud who did not actually start from nothing, as he so often claims, Dickens questions the validity of that entire justification for poverty. If the self-made man is a lie, then what can the poor hope to achieve? Moreover, Dickens raises the question of whether the self-made man owes anything to the rest of society. Are the wealthy under any obligation to help the poor? Or must the poor help themselves?

SUGGESTED ESSAY TOPICS

1. What is the significance of the book's structure? What does each of its three parts represent? Why are the different sections given agricultural titles when the book is about industrial England?

2. Does *Hard Times* have a protagonist? Does it have a main character? What makes you think so, and who might the main character be?

3. *Hard Times* begins and ends with a meeting between Mr. Sleary and Mr. Gradgrind. How are the meetings different? What changes in Mr. Gradgrind's character and values do we see between his first and last encounter with the circus folk?

4. Discuss the character of Stephen Blackpool. How does he represent the poor Hands in *Hard Times*? Do you think it is an accurate representation? Is it meant to be?

5. *Hard Times* is built around a few simple, contrasting thematic ideas. What are some of them, and how do they function in the book? How does Louisa fit among these ideas?

6. As a child, Bitzer is a model pupil at Gradgrind's school. How does his conduct as a porter at Bounderby's bank reflect his early education? Would you consider him a "success" according to Gradgrind's criteria? Why or why not?

REVIEW & RESOURCES

QUIZ

1. What is the name of Sissy's father's dog?

    A. Happylegs
    B. Bandylegs
    C. Merrylegs
    D. Mr. Snips

2. What is the main principle of Mr. Gradgrind's philosophy?

    A. Fact
    B. Fancy
    C. Love
    D. Patriotism

3. Mrs. Pegler is the mother of which character?

    A. Gradgrind
    B. Sissy
    C. Stephen
    D. Bounderby

4. Who robs the bank?

    A. Stephen
    B. Tom
    C. Sissy
    D. Mrs. Sparsit

5. What is the common name for poor Coketown factory workers?

    A. Cogs
    B. Scum
    C. Hands
    D. Proles

6. Sissy believes her father abandoned her for what reason?

    A.   Her own best interest

    B.   To elope with a Frenchwoman

    C.   Grief over her mother's death

    D.   A desire to see the world

7. Which of the following characters dies during the course of the novel?

    A.   Sleary

    B.   Mrs. Gradgrind

    C.   Gradgrind

    D.   James Harthouse

8. Who is Kidderminster?

    A.   A circus worker who dresses up as Cupid

    B.   Mr. Gradgrind's fellow Member of Parliament

    C.   Sissy's father

    D.   The Hand who organizes the workers' union

9. What does Rachael find that leads her to believe Stephen has been murdered?

    A.   A trail of bloody footprints

    B.   A note from the killer

    C.   His hat, abandoned in a field

    D.   An empty bottle of poison

10. How does Stephen die?

    A.   He is crushed by factory machinery

    B.   A fall into Old Hell Shaft

    C.   Murder

    D.   Malnutrition as a result of poverty

11. Who runs the circus?

    A.   Sleary

    B.   Bitzer

    C.   Mrs. Pegler

    D.   Sissy's father

12. About how much money is stolen from the bank?

    A. 150 pounds
    B. 3,000 pounds
    C. 40,000 pounds
    D. 128,000 pounds

13. Which character is a Member of Parliament?

    A. Bounderby
    B. Mr. McChoakumchild
    C. Bitzer
    D. Gradgrind

14. What is Bounderby's son's name?

    A. Bitzer
    B. Tom
    C. James Harthouse
    D. Bounderby has no son

15. In which city does most of the novel take place?

    A. Coketown
    B. Liverpool
    C. London
    D. Evenly divided between Coketown and London

16. From what does Mrs. Sparsit imagine Louisa falling?

    A. A ladder
    B. A staircase
    C. The opera balcony
    D. The moon

17. Who is the first character to speak in the novel?

    A. Bounderby
    B. Sissy
    C. Bitzer
    D. Gradgrind

18. Why is Stephen unable to marry Rachael?

    A.   He is already married
    B.   He is too old
    C.   He is too poor
    D.   She is in love with another man

19. How do the poor of Coketown attempt to improve
    their conditions?

    A.   By burning the factory
    B.   By looting the bank
    C.   By forming a union.
    D.   By petitioning Parliament for assistance.

20. What is the name of Mrs. Sparsit's aristocratic relative?

    A.   Col. Reginald Powler
    B.   Lady Scadgers
    C.   Rupert Hardwick, Esq.
    D.   Ephraim Gride

21. What does Gradgrind hope Tom will be able to do after
    Stephen's death?

    A.   Escape England
    B.   Move up at the bank
    C.   Marry Sissy
    D.   Inherit Stephen's fortune

22. What is Bitzer's defining characteristic?

    A.   His pale skin
    B.   His facial scar
    C.   His limp
    D.   His red hair

23. Where does Louisa flee after Harthouse's declaration
    of love?

    A.   Her husband's house
    B.   Her father's house
    C.   Stephen's room
    D.   The circus

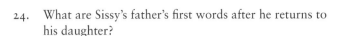

24. What are Sissy's father's first words after he returns to his daughter?

    A. "Oh, Sissy, how I've missed you!"
    B. "At last . . . at long last . . . my daughter. . . ."
    C. "Child, do you not know me at last?"
    D. He never returns

25. What motivates Harthouse to become one of Gradgrind's political disciples?

    A. He believes in Gradgrind's philosophy of fact
    B. Boredom
    C. The desire for wealth
    D. Pride

Answer Key:

1: C; 2: A; 3: D; 4: B; 5: C; 6: A; 7: B; 8: A; 9: C; 10: B;
11: A; 12: A; 13: D; 14: D; 15: A; 16: B; 17: D; 18: A; 19: C;
20: B; 21: A; 22: A; 23: B; 24: B; 25: B

SUGGESTIONS FOR FURTHER READING

ADRIAN, ARTHUR A. *Dickens and the Parent-Child Relationship.* Athens, Ohio: Ohio University Press, 1984.

BARNARD, ROBERT. *Imagery and Theme in the Novels of Dickens.* New York: Humanities Press, 1974.

BLOOM, HAROLD, ed. HARD TIMES *(Modern Critical Interpretations).* New York: Chelsea House, 1992.

GLANCY, RUTH. *Student Companion to Charles Dickens.* Greenwood, Connecticut: Greenwood Press, 1999.

HARDY, BARBARA. *The Moral Art of Dickens.* New York: Oxford University Press, 1970.

HIGBIE, ROBERT. *Dickens and Imagination.* Gainesville: University Press of Florida, 1998.

LEAVIS, F. R. and Q. D. LEAVIS. *Dickens the Novelist.* London: Chatto and Windus, 1970.

MACKENZIE, NORMAN and JEANNE MACKENZIE. *Dickens: A Life.* New York: Oxford University Press, 1979.

MANNING, SYLVIA BANK. *Dickens as Satirist.* New Haven: Yale University Press, 1971.

REVIEW & RESOURCES

A Note on the Type

The typeface used in SparkNotes study guides is Sabon, created by master typographer Jan Tschichold in 1964. Tschichold revolutionized the field of graphic design twice: first with his use of asymmetrical layouts and sanserif type in the 1930s when he was affiliated with the Bauhaus, then by abandoning assymetry and calling for a return to the classic ideals of design. Sabon, his only extant typeface, is emblematic of his latter program: Tschichold's design is a recreation of the types made by Claude Garamond, the great French typographer of the Renaissance, and his contemporary Robert Granjon. Fittingly, it is named for Garamond's apprentice, Jacques Sabon.

SPARKNOTES
TEST PREPARATION
GUIDES

The SparkNotes team figured it was time to cut standardized tests down to size. We've studied the tests for you, so that SparkNotes test prep guides are:

Smarter
Packed with critical-thinking skills and test-
taking strategies that will improve your score.

Better
Fully up to date, covering all new features of the tests,
with study tips on every type of question.

Faster
Our books cover exactly what you need to
know for the test. No more, no less.

SPARKNOTES™ LITERATURE GUIDES